Joseph
and the
Fearful
Family

To Megan

First published in Great Britain in 2018

Society for Promoting Christian Knowledge
36 Causton Street, London SW1P 4ST
www.spck.org.uk

British Library Cataloguing-in-Publication Data
A catalogue record for this book is available from the British Library

ISBN 978-0-281-07473-0

13 5 7 9 10 8 6 4 2

Typeset by Gill McLean
Printed in Great Britain by Ashford Colour Press

Produced on paper from sustainable forests

Joseph
and the
Fearful
Family

Fiona Veitch Smith

Illustrated by
Andy Catling

SPCK

Joseph was one of **twelve** brothers who used to live with their **dad** and stepmothers on a farm in the land of **Canaan**. There were sheep, goats and *lots* and **lots** of cows.

There were **fat** cows and **skinny** cows and somewhere-in-between cows, but **Joseph** loved them *all*.

Now, **Joseph** no longer
lived in **Canaan**.

His **brothers** –
who were **jealous**
of him because
their **father** had given
him a **rainbow** robe –
had been *very* **unkind** to him

But, eventually, he had been set free.
He was now
the **second most important person**
in Egypt, riding in a **chariot** beside Pharaoh.

and people **cheered** them both as they went by.

In those days there was a **famine** in Egypt and all the countries around. This meant that **not enough** food could be grown to feed everyone.

But **God** had told Joseph and Pharaoh through a **dream** that the **famine** was coming, so Joseph advised Pharaoh to **store up enough** food to last for **seven** years.

Pharaoh agreed and put Joseph in **charge** of it all.

Back in **Canaan**, however, no one had told **Joseph's family** that there was going to be a **famine**

so everyone on the old **farm** was **very hungry** indeed.

Joseph's dad, **Jacob**, sent **ten** of his **sons** down to **Egypt** to **buy some food,**

but kept the **youngest** boy, **Benjamin**, at home.

When the **brothers** arrived in **Egypt** to buy **grain**, they did not know that the **person in *charge*** was their brother **Joseph**.

Joseph, now dressed like an **Egyptian**, looked very different from the boy they had **teased** and **bullied** back home on the **farm**.

When **Joseph** saw his **ten brothers**,
he knew **immediately** who they were.

There was **Reuben** (the **strong** one),

Judah (the one they called '**Lion**')

Simeon and Levi (the **fighty** ones),

and Issachar (who **laughed** like a donkey).

Then there was Dan (the **peacemaker**),
Gad (the **chatterbox**),
Naphtali (the **shy** one),
Zebulun (the **fisherman**)
and Asher (the **cook**).

Dan

Gad Naphtali

Zebulun

Asher

The only one who was missing was the **youngest**, Benjamin.

Joseph smiled as he remembered what a **greedy** little boy he had been.

Joseph was still very **angry**
with his brothers, though,
because of the **horrible** things they had done to him
and he wanted them to **suffer** for a little bit longer.

He also wanted to see **Benjamin**,
so he **asked the brothers** about
their family back in **Canaan**,
pretending he didn't know *anything* about them.

Reuben told him their **father**
was still **alive**,
that they had a *younger* brother
and *another* brother who had **died**.

(They did not tell him that
they had sold him
as a **slave**.)

This made Joseph very **angry**.
'You are **lying** to me!
You are not here to buy **food**.
You are **spies**!' he said, and threw them into **jail**.

The **brothers** were very **sad**,
but agreed that they were finally being **punished**
for the **terrible** things they had done before.

After the *third* day,
Joseph let **nine** of his **brothers** go,
but kept Simeon in **prison**.

Then he said to them,
'To **prove** you are **not spies**,
you must **go back to Canaan**
and bring your **youngest brother** to me.
If you **return** I will know that you were *not* **lying**
and let Simeon go.'

So the **nine brothers** got on their **donkeys**
and **went home**.
When they arrived,
they told their **father** what had happened.
'We *must* take Benjamin back with us,' said **Reuben**.

'You shall **not** take him!' cried Jacob.
'Joseph is **dead** and Simeon is **lost**.
You shall **not** take Benjamin away from me, too.'

Nothing the **brothers** said could convince him to **change his mind**.

Back in **Egypt**, Joseph waited and **waited**, but the **brothers** did not come.

This made **Joseph** *very* **sad**.

He was tempted to visit Simeon in prison and tell him the **truth**, but he was still too angry.

Instead, he went back to his work and tried to **forget** his family and the beautiful **farm** in Canaan.

Also available in the Young Joseph series

Joseph and the Rainbow Robe
978-0-281-07468-6

Joseph and the Jealous Brothers
978-0-281-07469-3

Joseph and the Lying Lady
978-0-281-07470-9

Joseph and the Forgetful Servant
978-0-281-07471-6

Joseph and the Dreaming Pharaoh
978-0-281-0-7472-3

Joseph and the Hidden Cup
978-0-281-07474-7